Northview Media Center
marks on cover
4/99 QM

W9-AWP-277

DATE DUE

JAN 15 '98	MAR 21 2002	
FEB 17 '98	OCT 10 2002	
FEB 24 '98	JAN 28	OCT 10 '07
MAR 20 '98	FEB 24	
APR 28 '98	APR 06	
SEP 25 1998	APR 30	
OCT 01 1998	OCT 19	
NOV 2 1998		
NOV 18 1998	APR 11	
DEC 03 1998	AUG 31 '12	
APR 30 1999	SEP 22 '06	
MAY 14 1999	FEB 05 '07	
MAR 17 2000	FEB 19 '07	
NOV 1 2000	MAR 20 '07	
OCT 03 2001		
NOV 01 2001	APR 04 '07	
MAY 07 2002	APR '07	

HIGHSMITH #45230

Printed in USA

DELETED

NORTHVIEW MEDIA CENTER

T9052   796.21 SHO
Skateboarding streetstyle

Action Sports

Skateboarding Streetstyle

Joel Shoemaker

Capstone Press

MINNEAPOLIS

Copyright © 1995 Capstone Press. All rights reserved. No part of this book may be reproduced in any form without written permission from the publisher.

Printed in the United States of America.

Capstone Press • 2440 Fernbrook Lane • Minneapolis, MN 55447

Editorial Director   John Coughlan
Managing Editor   John Martin
Production Editor   James Stapleton
Copy Editor   Thomas Streissguth

Library of Congress Cataloging-in-Publication Data

Shoemaker, Joel.
   Skateboarding streetstyle / by Joel Shoemaker.
     p. cm. -- (Action sports)
   Includes bibliographical references and index.
   Summary: Presents the development of skateboarding since the 1920s as well as techniques of moving, turning, and stopping and the need for protective clothing and equipment.
   ISBN 1-56065-261-6
   1. Skateboarding--Juvenile literature. [1. Skateboarding.]
I. Title. II. Series.
GV859.8.S46 1995
796.21--dc20   95-7810
                                                    CIP
                                                    AC

99 98 97 96 95   6 5 4 3 2 1

Table of Contents

Chapter 1

Streetstyle Skateboarders

Streetstyle skateboarders come in many different shapes, sizes, and ages. But they all have certain things in common. They like to be outside. They like to be active. They're athletic, with balance, good control of their bodies, and quick reactions. And they're always ready to learn new moves.

Concrete and Asphalt

You can skateboard on driveways, sidewalks, schoolyards, parking lots, and other paved surfaces. Most streetstyle skateboarding

A good skateboarder know the best way to tackle any obstacle and stay under control.

is done on concrete and asphalt. The surface can be flat or curved, smooth or rough. It can slope up a bank or run along the top of a wall. Whatever the surface, streetstyle skateboarders can find a way to get over it.

Thinking Fast

Problems will come at you fast while skateboarding. So your mind and your body have to work fast as well. You'll keep a sharp eye out for obstacles and figure out the best way over, around, or through these dangers.

Every decision counts. If you skate the best line and miss the rocks, cracks, curbs, trash, and leaves, you roll on. Make a bad decision, and you'll faceplant (crash).

You'll float along the ground and feel the wind in your face. As you get better, you'll throw in some tricks to keep it interesting. You may be taking on a skatepark ramp or the curving sides of an empty pool. Or you may be traveling freestyle, all the way across town. Wherever you're going, you're free. And finding the best way to get there is the fun of streetstyle skateboarding.

Chapter 2

Getting a Skateboard

Skateboarding has been around a long time. In the 1920s and 1930s, skateboards were just roller skates nailed to a board. Their steel wheels were noisy. They couldn't turn, and they often skidded. Any rock or crack stopped them instantly.

The 1960s

In the 1960s, skateboards were small and flat. Compared to the boards now in use, they were heavy and stiff and didn't turn very well. But skateboarding was catching on fast. The

first international competition took place in
1965, in Anaheim, California.

In those days, skateboards had modern
trucks (wheel assemblies), but the wheels were
made of a hard material that skidded easily.
They gave better control than steel wheels, but
they stopped on small pebbles, twigs, and
cracks.

In 1972 came a revolution in skateboarding.
That was the year Frank Nasworthy invented
the urethane wheel. The new wheels made the
boards faster and the ride smoother and softer.
The better traction of urethane also made
hundreds of new tricks possible.

Better Boards

Today's skateboards are easier to maneuver.
The deck is made of maple plywood, six or
seven layers thick. Some decks are flat, but
most are molded to turn up at the tail and
sometimes at the nose. This makes the board
easier to move with your feet.

Modern decks are sturdy enough to take a lot of pounding, but they are also flexible. They can bend to absorb some of the impact from a jump or drop. To increase traction, a skater can glue grip tape, which has a rough surface like sandpaper, to the top of a board.

Trucks and Wheels

When the board is closer to the ground, it has a lower center of gravity. This makes it easier to do tricks. For this reason, trucks are getting lower and narrower, and the urethane wheels have a smaller diameter. They are soft enough to let the skater roll over small rocks and cracks, and yet are durable enough to last a long time. High-quality axles and bearings also offer good reliability, speed, and control.

Paint Jobs

New boards have fantastic paint jobs that appear on the bottom of the deck. You can always find one that fits you. Or, you can buy a unpainted deck and do it yourself. Blank decks are also cheaper than prepainted decks.

Chapter 3

Getting Started

If you have never skateboarded before, visit a shop that sells skateboards. You'll get some advice about the kind of board that's right for you. The sales people can recommend a board that fits your size, the kind of skating you want to do, and how much money you have to spend.

At the same time, you should buy some protective clothing (helmet, knee pads, elbow pads, wrist pads, and gloves). This equipment is often sold for other wheeled sports, like inline skating. Wearing it will improve your chances of having fun with little pain.

Take Time

There are several exercises that will get you ready for streetstyle skateboarding. They may take you a single afternoon, or you might need several sessions over many days or weeks. There's no rush—take the time you need. The more carefully you learn the basics, the better skater you'll be.

Balance

It is important to get a feel for your new board. Find a smooth, paved surface that is free of all traffic. Put the board in one spot, and practice getting on and off the board. Stand still on the board.

Experiment by carefully shifting your weight forward and back. Then shift from side to side. Try bending your knees slightly. Notice how you have to adjust the rest of your body to keep from falling off.

Don't try jumps until you're sure of your footing and balance on the board.

These moves are not easy—you may have to practice for awhile. Take your time. If you learn them well, it will help you do the next steps more easily.

Getting Moving

Now you're ready to move. Place one foot near the centerline of the board, over or slightly in back of the front trucks. Push off with the foot that's still on the ground. Don't

This expert knows the fastest way down a railing.

While in flight, always keep your weight centered over the board.

try to put this foot on the board yet. Let it sweep forward and push off again. Practice balancing on the board this way, with one foot on the board and one foot off.

Try the same with the other foot on the board. This will help you find your most natural stance. Try standing still, bending your knees, and shifting your weight while moving

the skateboard slowly across the pavement.
You'll soon be ready to turn.

Turning

The simplest way to turn the skateboard is to
tilt the deck in the direction you want to turn. If
you tilt it to the left, you turn left. If you tilt it
to the right, you turn right. You can sharpen the
turns by leaning into them.

Stopping

Most skateboards have no brakes, so
stopping will be a challenge. Practice by
stepping off the board in a running motion, so
that you can kick the board backwards slightly
as you leave it. This keeps it from rolling ahead
of you and running into someone. Depending
on your speed, you should be able to come to a
stop in a few steps.

A bail is a step off the board. When you
practice stepping off the board, you're learning
how to bail safely and under control.

Chapter 4

Good Moves

At first, going down a gentle slope in a straight line is hard enough. With practice, you'll have the easy moves down cold. As you get more confident, you'll start going faster, leaning into turns, and trying some tricks. Once you've learned some tricks, there's no end to the fun you can have.

Wheelies and Kickturns

Wheelies are the first tricks many riders learn. You ride on the back or front wheels only, usually for a short distance or as part of another trick.

The basic rear wheelie can be a good way to stop. You drag the tail of the deck and the heel of your shoe on the surface. This creates enough friction to stop the skateboard.

The wheelie is also a basic part of other moves. For example, a kickturn is a wheelie that changes your direction. To do a kickturn, begin by pulling a wheelie. With the nose of the board raised, swing the board to the left or right with your front foot and then lower the nose back to the ground.

A 90° kickturn changes your direction one-quarter of a turn. A 180° kickturn reverses your direction. And a 360° kickturn is a complete spin that leaves you going the same way as when you started.

Drops and Ollies

Drops from one level to a lower one, such as from a sidewalk to the street, are another basic move. To drop, lift the front wheels up as you leave the edge, shift your back foot forward over the axle, and flex your knees to push the board down for the landing.

You can get over obstacles with an ollie. To do an ollie, you push down on the tail of the board while jumping into the air. With practice, you can keep the board under control while you come back down on top of the deck. The ollie is the best move there is for catching air —getting the board completely off the ground. It's fun to do and spectacular to see.

There are a lot of variations, including the ollie 180 (reversing the direction of your

A clean ollie will get you over almost any obstacle.

Fast footwork lets you flip the board in mid-air—the classic kickflip move.

body), and the ollie 360 (spinning completely around one revolution). To do an ollie kickflip, the skater uses fast footwork to spin the board completely around. The ollie endover flips the board end over end.

In an ollie nosepick, the skateboarder first climbs up the side of a curb. He then grabs the side of the board, jumps just above the deck, then angles back down to the pavement in one smooth motion.

Slides and Grinds

There are many kinds of slides, including noseslides, tailslides, and railslides. To slide, you skid the board along a surface more or less sideways to the direction of travel. Most slides are done with the bottom of the board against a surface like a curb. If the surface is slick enough, some slides can be done on the wheels.

After you've perfected your low slides, you can ollie higher surfaces like benches and railings and use them for slides of various types. In a front-side slide, you are facing the same direction you are moving. In a back-side slide, you are going backwards.

The grind is one way to tackle a ramp or the lip of a pool. In a frontside grind, for example, the skater lifts the back of the board up onto the edge of a ramp. The back axle slides along the edge as the skater turns the front around, then heads back down the ramp.

30

As the tricks get harder, skateboarders use grabs more often to help keep control. This means using your hands to hold the board in position while catching air.

New Moves

Streetstyle skateboarders are inventing new moves all the time. One of the most exciting is the wallie. A wallie is an ollie that sends you straight up the side of a wall, then back down again. It's as hard as it looks!

In the no comply, the skater plants his front foot on the ground and spins the board around with his back foot. The tail turns to the front, the nose faces the rear, and the skater keeps going—while facing the other way.

The fastplant has to be done at high speed. The skater ollies up and onto an obstacle, grabs the edge of the board, and plants his back foot. The foot quickly pushes off again, and the skater's weight carries the board back down to the pavement.

Equipment

For streetstyle tricks, skaters keep the bushings loose for maximum control in tight-turning, slow-speed moves. For fast, downhill and slalom skating, most skaters tighten the trucks down to reduce the chance of shimmies. Be sure to practice with an easy, short run when adjusting your trucks. Otherwise you can expect a serious case of road rash.

Skateboarders can get airborne easily—but watch out. What goes up must come down!

Balance and control are the key to good streetstyle skateboarding.

Speed or Tricks?

For some streetstyle skateboarders, the best thing about their sport is the speed. For others, the fun is figuring out how to do the acrobatic tricks and moves of freestyle and ramp skateboarding. The best streetstyle move is one that gets you where you want to go, safely and in your own style.

Chapter 5

Staying in Control

Good skateboarding means staying in control. If you're moving fast in a straight line, especially downhill, you're probably out of control. Carving turns back and forth across the pavement is the best way to keep good control.

Judging Conditions

You can get hurt by moving faster than is safe for the conditions. You also have to judge things like changing light and visiblity, how well your skateboard is gripping the surface,

A good kickflip takes good timing. If the board doesn't land right, neither will you.

the movements of people and vehicles, and the height of drops.

Outlaw Skateboarding

Streetstyle skateboarding is banned in many places because of obnoxious behavior by some skaters. It is important for streetstyle skaters to obey posted laws. Outlaw skating hurts everyone who wants to keep skating streetstyle. Always avoid places where skateboarding is illegal. There's plenty of legal pavement out there to conquer.

A concrete slope can get you moving in a hurry.

Chapter 6
Getting Hurt

Broken bones, pulled muscles, damaged tendons, and bloody scrapes can happen anytime. You can be seriously and permanently injured while skateboarding.

The dangers increase when you skateboard among motorcycles, cars, trucks, and buses. So don't do it. Skate in safe environments. Avoid traffic, stay alert, and skate again tomorrow.

Good Attitude

Skateboarding can be dangerous, and that's why it probably drives your parents crazy. It may also be one of the reasons you like to do it. You like the risk, and the challenge.

You may also enjoy learning to do something new, something you couldn't do yesterday. Remember—the way to learn a new skateboarding move is to try it, over and over again, until you get it right. Hundreds of tries may be necessary. A never-say-die attitude is what separates the winner from the quitter.

Moving On

It's great to skate with friends. What good is doing a fantastic move if there's no one to see it? You'll want to laugh and brag about it. Showing a friend how to do a new move is fun. And watching someone else shred a new piece of pavement can help you learn something new.

Your skateboarding skills will grow with you. As you get better at it, you'll enjoy learning new moves and harder tricks. In streetstyle skateboarding, the fun and challenge never stop.

Glossary

axles–metal shafts that the wheel and bearings spin around

bail–leaving the board under control

bearings–ball bearings that reduce friction between the axle and other parts of the truck

blank–an unpainted skateboard deck

bushings–rubber grommets on the truck that can be adjusted to make turning easier or harder

centerline–an imaginary line down the center of the skateboard deck

clean–used to describe a trick or move that is well done

deck–a skateboard's top surface, usually made of plywood

downhill–skating down a big incline, trying to go as fast as possible

drop–to move from a higher level to a lower one, as from a step, bench, or ledge down to a sidewalk

faceplant–an uncontrolled crash; a fall that goes all the way down, especially if it's forward, or face-first

freestyle–working purely on moves, generally on a flat surface such as a new parking lot or basketball court

grab–a move using a hand on the board to keep control or assist in turning

grip tape–a sandpaper-like surface glued to the top of a board to increase traction

kickturn–to change direction by doing a wheelie and moving the airborne end of the board to a new position before lowering it to the ground

nose–the front end of the skateboard deck

ollie–a no-hands aerial. At a comfortable speed, pop the board up from the tail and maintain control with the feet

railslide–a move where you approach a fixed object like a curb, railing, or bench, then ollie onto it with the board turned 90 degrees (sideways) to slide along the edge

road rash–scraped and damaged skin from falling and sliding on the pavement

shimmies–when wheels shake back and forth quickly, causing a wobble that can make control difficult

shredding–aggressive skateboarding, such as carving hard turns and moving quickly through a slalom

slalom–carving turns to the left and right around cans or cones placed on a downhill pavement

slide–wheels skidding sideways; also sliding on a rail or obstacle, such as a curb, on the underside of the board, nose, tail, or trucks

tail–the back end of the skateboard deck, behind the rear trucks

trucks–the whole wheel assembly, typically made up of the baseplate, hanger, bushings, axle, grommet, pin, bearings, wheels, spacers, nuts, and bolts

urethane–a soft plastic material used to make wheels

wheelie–skating on the rear or front set of wheels only

To Learn More

Andrejtschitsch, Jan. *Action Skateboarding*. New York: Sterling, 1993.

Evans, Jeremy. *Skateboarding*. New York: Crestwood House, 1994.

Wilkins, Kevin. *Skateboarding*. Running Press, 1994.

Magazines

TransWorld SKATEboarding
P.O. Box 469006
Escondido, CA 92046

Video

License to Skate. Pantheon Industries, 1989.
Videorecording.

> Volume 1: *The Basics.*
>
> Volume 2: *Freestyle.*
>
> Volume 3*: Freestyle and Bankriding.*
>
> Volume 4: *Vertical and Stunts.*
>
> Volume 5: *Pointers on Competition.*
>
> Volume 6: *Equipment, Clothing,*

Photo Credits

©Grant Britain 1992: p. 26; 1993: pp. 6, 8, 10, 11, 19, 20, 21, 23; 1994: pp. 4, 28, 31, 34, 37, 40. ©Shawn Frederick: pp. 16, 29, 32. Jeff Kendall: pp. 13, 14, 24, 35, 36

Index

Northern Music Center

Northview Media Center